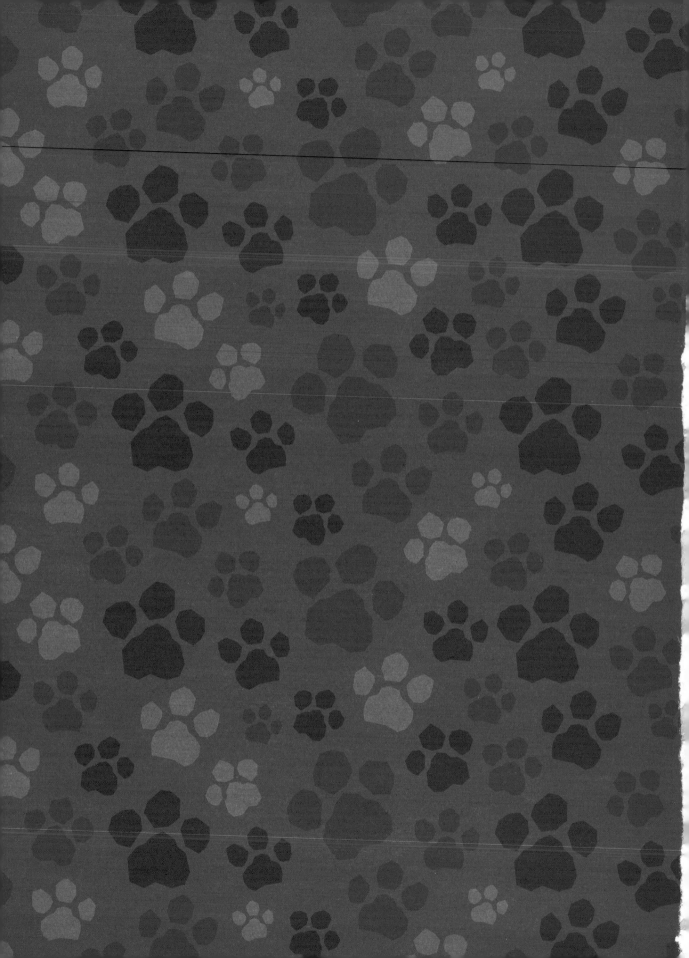

REAL RESCUE
DOGS
AND MORE ANIMAL HEROES!

CONTENTS

Amazing Animals!

Hero Spotlights!

The pups of PAW Patrol are always ready to save the day! In communities everywhere, dogs pitch in to make the world a safer place. Check out the different jobs that these incredible dogs do and how they help those around them every day!

FIREFIGHTER DOGS

Dogs have been helping firefighters for 300 years!

Before gas-powered trucks were invented, dogs used to run out of the firehouse first. They would bark and make sure everyone got out of the way for the horse and carriage.

Today, dogs go with firefighters to schools to help teach about fire safety.

This fire pup is suited up!

POLICE DOGS

Dogs help the police in many different ways.

Lots of police dogs are German Shepherds. German Shepherds are great at protecting people and finding missing stuff with their super sniffers!

This police dog has his own badge!

Hero Spotlight!

Toby the Heimlich Dog

When this Golden Retriever saw that his owner couldn't breathe, he leapt into action! Toby knocked her onto the ground and jumped on her chest, in a doggy-version of the Heimlich maneuver. The piece of apple dislodged and everyone was alright!

What a
handy
pup to
have
around!

AIRPORT SECURITY DOGS

These dogs sniff our luggage!

When you visit another country, there are some things like animals or fresh produce that you can't bring home. Dogs can use their excellent sense of smell to sniff out items that are not allowed in luggage.

This beagle's nose knows what's in the bag!

Hero Spotlight!

Piper the Runway Patrol Dog

Piper works at an airport and he has every dog's dream job: Barking at birds all day! Piper keeps birds off the runway so they don't get in the way of landing planes.

What a useful pup!

This pup's goggles protect his eyes!

SLED DOGS

These dogs pull sleds through snow!

Nowadays most sled dogs are used for racing, but they can also carry all sorts of things, like mail, supplies and even people!

Sled dogs have been used for a really long time in places with too much snow for cars!

What a
team!

HERDING DOGS

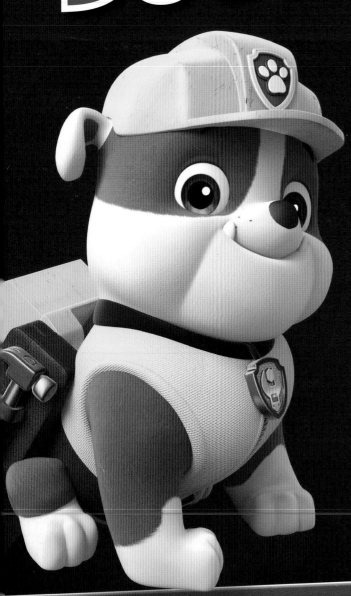

These dogs round up other animals!

Herding dogs help farmers move livestock, such as sheep or goats! They also make sure the animals they're rounding up don't stray into the road or get separated from the pack.

Herding dogs keep the herd safe!

This pup knows how to work a crowd!

GUIDE DOGS

These dogs help people get around!

Guide dogs aid people who are blind or visually impaired. These service dogs guide their owners across the street and help them avoid obstacles!

Golden Retrievers make great guide dogs!

Guide dogs wear harnesses!

Hero Spotlight!

LilyBelle the Goldendoodle

LilyBelle is a super special service dog! Her owner, Meghan, has a very severe nut allergy. Thankfully, LilyBelle keeps her safe— she uses her sense of smell to detect traces of nuts in any food she is about to eat.

Now that's a protective pup!

What a special bond!

THERAPY DOGS

These dogs bring comfort and happiness.

There are lots of therapy dogs who visit patients in hospitals, schools and nursing homes. When people spend time with therapy dogs, they report feeling more joy.

Pups make people happy!

Pups are the best medicine!

SEARCH AND RESCUE DOGS

They find missing and lost people!

Search and rescue dogs smell with their noses and listen with their ears to find people lost in the wilderness or who got trapped after a natural disaster, like a hurricane or an avalanche.

I'm all ears!

This pup is on the trail!

Hero Spotlight!

Wilson the Doberman Pinscher Pup

Wilson was walking on the beach with his owner, Richard, when he began to bark extra loud. A man was having trouble getting back to shore! Richard alerted a lifeboat station, and the man was rescued.

Ready, set, get wet!

This pup was ready to dive in!

MILITARY DOGS

These dogs help soldiers!

Military dogs are really tough! Only about half of official military dogs make it through their training. They need to be in perfect health and be highly reward motivated— that means they'll do anything for a treat!

These pups are ready for a ruff ruff rescue!

This pup is ready for duty!

Pups
are
amazing!

Remember, whenever you're in trouble, just yelp for help!

Media Lab Books
For inquiries, call 646-838-6637

Copyright 2017 Topix Media Lab

Published by Topix Media Lab
14 Wall Street, Suite 4B
New York, NY 10005

Printed in China

ISBN-10: 1-942556-70-5
ISBN-13: 978-1-942556-70-1